To Radim

Thank you for
inspiring me!

Sarah Ellen

:)

BEING THE REAL YOU

A handbook of quotes and reflections
to inspire you on life's journey

Sarah Ellen Masters

First published in the United Kingdom in 2019 by
Sarah Ellen Masters, www.sarahellenmasters.com.

Being the Real You - A handbook of quotes and reflections
to inspire you on life's journey ©2019 Sarah Ellen Masters

1 2 3 4 5 6 7 8 9 10 / 23 22 21 20 19

Written, compiled and designed by Sarah Ellen Masters
Copyediting by Emily Gosling

ISBN 978-1-9160976-0-5

To find out more about this publication or the author,
please visit sarahellenmasters.com.

ATTENTION + CONNECTION = CREATION

Our ability to make connections has an impact on our entire life experience. I believe that true connections are born through focus.

Now that social media plays such a prominent role in our lives, we're beginning to see that behind the shiny screens and heart emojis, it isn't all likes and fun. Evidence is building for its detrimental effect on our mental health, wellbeing, time and ability to interact with others. Technology will never be able to replace real human connection.

Wherever you're at in your life at the moment, to begin the process of creating – and being the real you – you have to get to grips with what it truly means to be in the moment, and as such, to connect with the world around you.

ATTENTION

CONTENTS

CONNECTION

CREATION

INTRODUCTION

This book is created for everyone: its focus is to shine a light on your journey into becoming and being the real you.

This book is divided into three categories: Attention, Connection and Creation. The passages I have written alongside each set of quotes are like the excerpts from a journal I never had – mostly things I wish I'd known sooner, but that I've realised take time, experience and reflection to truly understand.

I'm always amazed at how a powerful quotation can provide encouragement, new insights, motivation and even permission to break free from a harmful set of circumstances. The right quotation is like a ray of sunshine that lifts your spirits and radiates a positive light through your mind and heart.

Gathering these quotes together over the years has shown me there's a common thread that seems to run through them all: those profound thoughts have made a difference to people's lives. In becoming the best version of you, however, I believe it's important to formulate your own opinions: these words are merely there to accelerate you in the right direction.

The texts here have all guided me in times of hardship – brought me to truth and helped me to focus my mind on the positive. They continue to alter the way I look at the world, and I believe they will change your life too.

My invitation is for you to read, reflect and respond; put them to use and follow their example. The aim of this book is to inspire and motivate you, restore hope and occasionally make you smile.

The quotes chosen are assembled from many sources and time periods. I have done my best to correctly attribute each quote to its original author, however, some quotes have been attributed to various people over the years.

Sarah Ellen Masters

HOW TO GET THE MOST OUT OF THIS BOOK

This book has been designed for reference in tricky times.
You could:

1. Read from beginning to end, pausing and reflecting on the pages that resonate the most with you at this stage in your journey.

2. Read a quote each morning, and allow the words to be an inspiration for the day ahead. Write a quote down, take it with you, read it often and reflect upon it with each action you take that day. Give yourself a few minutes each evening to write any thoughts, ideas and feelings that come to you alongside the quote. You will be astonished at what eureka moments you might have.

3. Enjoy your book as a collection of inspirational quotes.

WHAT IS ATTENTION?

Attention is defined as "Notice taken of someone or something;
the regarding of someone or something as interesting or important; the mental
faculty of considering or taking notice of someone or something; and the
action of dealing with or taking special care of someone or something."

It takes skill and discipline to pay attention to the moment we are in, and
willpower to block out the overwhelming noise of the world. Attention is strong
and active – it connects us with others, it gives us passion – and if we're
attentive, we see the detailed beauty and magic each passing moment holds.

Giving attention to those around us is a simple action that can offer us
incredible happiness. Listening to others and understanding what they're
saying shows that we respect and value them as people, offering them their
own happiness in return.

Pouring ourselves completely and intentionally into the present moment and
paying attention each and every day of our lives brings us deeper, more
meaningful interactions.

**ROCK SOLID
PRINCIPLES**

In matters of principals,
stand like a rock;
in matters of taste,
swim with the current.

Thomas Jefferson,
Third President of the United States

ROCK SOLID PRINCIPLES

Sometimes, it's hard to know what we really want.
Giving time to think about what's important to us and setting our own set of personal principles to implement can make daily decisions less tricky.

Principles start with awareness, then the active choice to start a new habit. It takes effort to consistently work at enforcing personal principles – simple things like showing kindness, preparation for the day ahead or being appreciative are easy to do, but also pretty difficult. Without a set of principles, it's easy for us to lose direction.

Once we've created our own set, we can adapt them as we grow, all the while staying true to what we know is right.

What do you want to be known for? Your honesty? Integrity? Concern for others? Accountability? Passion for what you do? Your ability to give more than you take? How you value your time more than your money? How you avoid unnecessary negativity?

Practice implementing your chosen principles until they become habits that are built into your subconscious mind.

Unease, anxiety, tension, stress, worry — all forms of fear — are caused by too much future, and not enough presence.

Guilt, regret, resentment, grievances, sadness, bitterness, and all forms of non-forgiveness are caused by too much past, and not enough presence.

Ekhart Tolle,
spiritual teacher and author

LET GO

Let go of unnecessary pain.

Endless thinking without action achieves nothing. The only effect of anticipating bad things to come and worrying about past mistakes is suffering. If we have no control over what has already happened, or what we imagine could go wrong one day, then why do we suffer now?

You might have encountered unimaginable hardships in your life; and dark thoughts that try to persuade you that you're meant to go on suffering. Remember, you do deserve to be happy.

We have the ability to choose whether we engage with these negative thoughts or focus on the moment in hand.

TAP INTO THE MIRACLE OF NOW

Wherever you are, be there.
If you can be fully present now,
you'll know what it means to live.

Steve Goodier,
religious minister

TAP INTO THE MIRACLE OF NOW

It takes time to change the habit of flitting our minds from the past and future. Choosing to adapt so that we can enjoy each moment, every day, is what it is to truly live.

Here are a few ideas to help us stay rooted in the now:

Give away unneeded possessions; minimalism forces us to live in the now. Getting rid of items that we identify with past memories will liberate us from living in the past and help our minds to stay focused on the now.

Be grateful for the little things today, using all the senses to soak in what's around us: the skies we see, the things we touch, the tastes that excite us and the noises that stimulate us.

Forgive past hurts and resentments. We can't control the harm others have done to us, but we can control its impact on today.

Try switching your device to airplane mode. Take a break for a spot of cloud-gazing and admire how leaves dance in the wind. This is an unbeatable way to bring us back into the now and restore peace.

Set personal goals, but don't allow dreaming about the future to replace living today. What we focus and work hard on now will expand into all our futures. The best way to create the tomorrow we want is to focus on the today we have.

HOW TO BE

Your personal philosophy is the
greatest determining factor
in how your life works out.

Jim Rohn,
American entrepreneur, author
and motivational speaker

HOW TO BE

Our personal philosophy is like an operating system which allows us to make better decisions: it gives us the ability to think, process ideas and put to good use our existing knowledge. Developing our own personal philosophy will help order and strengthen our lives, shaping our purpose.

It's easy to not take ownership of our own philosophy. We must sort through all the knowledge we have acquired and put to good use the values and ideas that will take us places, both mentally and physically. Take responsibility of discarding negative thoughts; and use the values and ideas that are already there to cultivate a legacy that in a small way, might make the world a better place.

Mastery of philosophy is a matter of how to be, not how to do.

PURPOSE

The two most important days in your life are the day you were born and the day you find out why.

Mark Twain,
American writer

PURPOSE

Even the most meticulous planning doesn't guarantee success.
However, without a plan it is a certainty that we won't succeed at all.
When we have no clarity in our intentions, how will we know what
to do with our days? How will we know if we've achieved personal
accomplishments? How will we know when we've gone off track?

Purpose will often develop over the course of our lives. It could come from
a talent or a connection we have with others; and it's important to have fun
while we're searching for what we value most.

Other people can bring clarity to what our purpose is. Reading, for
instance, allows us to connect with another person's thoughts from any
background, time or culture. It could spark an idea or a curiosity that might
lead us to what matters most in our lives.

When we choose to be still, clear our minds and focus on declaring our
intentions, we are able to direct and prioritise our actions – actions that will
keep us on track towards what is really important to us.

SETTING PERSONAL BOUNDARIES

When we fail to set boundaries and
hold people accountable,
we feel used and mistreated.

Brené Brown,
author and public speaker

SETTING PERSONAL BOUNDARIES

We only get one shot at each day of our lives.
Our time can be gobbled up by so many things we shouldn't feel obliged to do, so let's pay more attention to how often we say "no".

It's ok for us to say no – when we do it nicely.

Being clear about what's important to us will make it easier for us to say no to what isn't essential. There are plenty of ways in which we can serve others without pushing ourselves to depletion and unhappiness.

Nobody else can set our personal boundaries for us. It's an act of self preservation: boundaries represent self awareness, and if we choose to respect our own, others should too.

RESPOND TO
DARKNESS

Courage is an inner resolution
to go forward in spite of obstacles
and frightening situations.

Martin Luther King, Jr,
American Baptist minister and activist

RESPOND TO DARKNESS

When was the last time you did something you were afraid of?
Fear is emotionally draining: it prevents us from living a life of
abundance and restricts us to a life of mediocrity.

All creative, smart people must fight fear every day — fear of failure,
fear of judgement, fear of not belonging. But as we distance ourselves
from our fears by observing them, and not owning them we can
change our behaviour and response to situations.

There will always be areas in which we're weaker than others, but it's
vital not to dwell on these and to focus on our strengths. Choosing to
face our fears will reap rewards in self-respect and happiness.

FILL UP WITH THE GOOD VIBES

My life – my personality, my habits, even my speech – is a combination of the books I choose to read, the people I choose to listen to, and the thoughts I choose to tolerate in my mind.

Andy Andrews,
American author and speaker

FILL UP WITH THE GOOD VIBES

Rubbish in, rubbish out: that which we choose to let into our minds shapes our souls for better or for worse.

Our quality of life depends on careful decision-making each and every day. If we're attentive to our thoughts and actions, we can make the most out of life and empower others to do the same.

Just as we choose to feed our bodies with nutritious foods, let's be as attentive to giving the best nutrition to our minds.

Make a conscious effort to shift habits: if watching crap TV late at night makes you feel negative, choose to call a friend instead, listen to a pre-sleep meditation podcast, watch a light hearted film or read a novel you love.

Thoughts shape our actions; actions shape our lives.

ADAPTING OUR PERSPECTIVE

To change ourselves effectively, we first had to change our perceptions.

Stephen R. Covey,
American author,
businessman and speaker

ADAPTING OUR PERSPECTIVE

Life is uncertain. At times it can be painful and soul crushing.
Dark times in our lives are an opportunity for us to grow. We naturally
want to know everything that's ahead and be in control. So when we
find out we've been duped, we feel empty and low. But if we want our
lives to change, we have to be open to thinking differently.

At different stages in our lives we face important decisions that will
dictate the direction we take. With the right attitude, changes can be
a healing process and an opportunity to develop. How we look at the
world and perceive our lives will make a huge difference in whether
we accept and grow, or resist and prolong our suffering.

Allowing ourselves to enjoy and receive life's pleasures will inspire and
uplift us, and give us a greater perspective on what's really important.
Look at things from every angle: consider facts, intuition, the guidance
of others.

Let's be more open and receptive to see the world through somebody
else's eyes; while also finding balance in giving ourselves time to
withdraw, be still and reflect.

TRAINING
OUR FOCUS

The successful warrior is the average man,
with laser-like focus.

Bruce Lee,
Martial artist and actor

TRAINING OUR FOCUS

Our ability to focus is not a talent or something we are born with.
Focus is a muscle, and it's our choice whether we use and develop
it or not.

Technology doesn't aid focus. How many times do we pick up our
phones and find ourselves procrastinating? It's hard to understand
how much time each week we spend aimlessly scrolling through other
peoples lives until we switch off – literally. Do we really need to be
entertained in every second?

As Cal Newport wrote in his book, Deep Work: Rules for Focused
Success in a Distracted World: "To simply wait and be bored has
become a novel experience in modern life, but from the perspective of
concentration training, it's incredibly valuable."

Each day, let's choose to master the simple act of staying on task, doing
whatever it is we need or intend to do. A sharper mind will give us
clarity, improve our decision making, and build our competence and
self-confidence.

We can learn to exercise our willpower, perhaps by only answering
emails at a set time in our day. We make our own rules. We'll discover
quickly how our days become so much more productive and enjoyable
when we are the ones in charge of tech, not the other way round.

RIDDING OURSELVES
OF WORRY

Worry a little bit every day and in a life-
time you will lose a couple of years.
If something is wrong, fix it if you can.
But train yourself not to worry.
Worry never fixes anything.

Ernest Hemingway,

writer

RIDDING OURSELVES OF WORRY

Worry is a useless habit, and a waste of our imaginations.
Earl Nightingale's The Essence of Success offers some stats on what most people worry about:

40% Things that never happen.
30% Things that have already happened.
12% Imagined health problems.
10% Petty worries about what other people think.
(any of the above we can't do anything about.)
8% Legitimate concerns that we can do something about.

What is it we've been worrying about? Is it something that a year from now we'll even remember? A little worry is good. After all, it pushes us into action. But too much can have a damaging impact on our health and happiness. We can choose to conquer our self-limiting negative thoughts by combating them with positive, logical ones. Writing down, speaking about and sharing our worries helps us to gain perspective.

If our worries stem from external events that we have no control over, we need to remember we have control over how we view those things we can't change. Focus on what is within our power to change.

When worry creeps in and we find ourselves getting anxious, we just have to ask ourselves: why am I feeling edgy and nauseous? Who's in control? Me or my fears?

Let's keep our worries in perspective.

LIVING WITH INTEGRITY

Integrity: the virtue of
being good without being watched.

Anonymous

LIVING WITH INTEGRITY

Why would we not choose to act in a way that is consistent with our core values? Integrity is about choosing courage over faint-heartedness; what's right over personal gain and instant gratification; and practicing our values instead of simply stating them.

Paying attention to our values and purpose will allow us to make smarter daily decisions that are in line with the person we are and the life that we want to create, whatever others' expectations might be.

It's inspiring when we take ownership of every decision we have made in the past — good or bad — and realise that the more we respect ourselves the higher we can raise others around us. This doesn't mean we can't make mistakes, but that when we own our decisions we can learn from them.

Why don't we focus on growing healthy positive relationships which are built on foundations of trust, respect, a commitment to understanding and to meeting the needs of others as best we can?

While it won't always be easy, we all know deep down that living with integrity is vital for inner peace and making decisions effectively, and well.

HEATHILY STRIVING TO
BE THE BEST YOU

When we strive to become better
than we are, everything around us
becomes better too.

Paulo Coelho,
Brazilian lyricist and novelist

HEATHILY STRIVING TO BE THE BEST YOU

Success is the total of our personal growth. When we set our own benchmarks and focus our energy on self improvement — continuing to learn and practice for ourselves, rather than looking at what others are doing – we create our own opportunities.

Let's choose to invest in our personal development: commit to reading influential books, attending seminars, and working alongside mentors and people with the same positive attitude; always continuing a lifelong journey of learning, growing and nurturing our potential. As American entrepreneur, author and speaker Jim Rohn said: "Don't wish it were easier, wish you were better. Don't wish for less problems, wish for more skills."

No one has all the answers, but we can learn the most when we're willing to work outside of our comfort zone and explore new things – the smallest piece of knowledge may spark a life changing idea when the time is right.

SETTING GOALS FOR
THE RIGHT REASONS

Too many people spend money they haven't earned, to buy things they don't want, to impress people they don't like.

Will Smith,
American actor

SETTING GOALS
FOR THE RIGHT REASONS

When was the last time you set a personal goal that was purely to prove something to yourself and nobody else?

Goals oriented around gaining the approval of others are meaningless. Are you motivated by other people's perception of you? A year from now will you remember or even care that you received a hundred likes on a social media post?

If we want true satisfaction, we've got to be smart and set goals for ourselves. Whatever it is, we will feel far more happiness and a sense of who we really are if we've listened to our hearts and not to our ego when progressing towards a goal.

By working hard on ourselves, for ourselves, we will develop self confidence, strength, self awareness and endurance. We will be liberated in the truth that we don't need to have anyone else's approval. Going to extreme lengths to impress someone else is insanity.

Do what you love and love what you do. Pay attention to what motivates you; create a goal that inspires you.

CHOICES THAT ILLUMINATE WHO WE ARE

Choices are the hinges of destiny.

Edwin Markham,
American poet

CHOICES THAT ILLUMINATE WHO WE ARE

Our choices will illuminate who we truly are.
Throughout our lives we will have times of adversity and times of advantage. Through the highs and the painful rock bottoms, there's one thing that will always stay consistent: our freedom of choice.

It's important to reflect on our decisions, learning from our bad choices and being proud of our good ones.

Nobody knows everything, and none of us can be the best at everything. Seeking out the views and experiences of others when we're outside of our comfort zones will help us to make more informed decisions.

The philosopher Voltaire warned against letting the perfect be the enemy of the good, so we must consider our own intuition when taking action. Procrastination rarely aids effective decision making.

We're only human, so once we've made a decision, we can't look back – we've got to make it work to the best of our ability. We can't change the past, so let's not waste time and energy thinking about what could have been different.

STRENGTHENING COMMITMENTS

Unless commitment is made,
there are only promises and hopes...
but no plans.

Peter F. Drucker,
American-Austrian educator and author

STRENGTHENING COMMITMENTS

We make commitments with others and ourselves everyday.
At the time, we fully intend to keep those commitments, but life can get in the way – we get tied up with other plans and before we know it those commitments are broken. It helps to write things down, to help us stick to our promises, whether big or small: they have ripple effects throughout our lives and often those of others too.

There are always ways to strengthen our commitments: focus on clear and realistic intentions, make a plan, engage with supportive people, draw up a list of your own motivations for change and a list of what you are willing to sacrifice in order to attain your goals. Would you give up seeing your friends every other weekend to achieve a promotion? Make those sort of choices ahead of time to avoid temptation. You'll be surprised how committing to one goal can have a positive impact on so many other areas of your life.

LET US BE
THE CHANGE

Change will not come if we wait for some other person or some other time.
We are the one's we've been waiting for.
We are the change we seek.

Barack Obama,
Former President of the United States

LET US BE THE CHANGE

If there is something we feel passionately about changing or contributing to in this world, let's not wait. Nobody is coming to do the job for us. When a seed is planted in our hearts and minds it's our duty to take responsibility.

We can be accountable for our own greatness and designing the change we want to see in the world. Entrepreneur, author and motivational speaker Jim Rohn put it best: "For things to change, you have to change. For things to get better, you have to get better. For things to improve, you have to improve."

Start with daily actions: notice what happens around you as your day unfolds today, and choose to act with kindness and compassion towards others. Positive actions are contagious. Stop waiting for others to change things and be the leader you've been waiting for.

**SELF DISCIPLINE
= SELF RESPECT**

Small disciplines repeated
with consistency every day lead to great
achievements gained slowly over time.

John C. Maxwell,
American author, speaker and pastor

SELF DISCIPLINE = SELF RESPECT

Most of us acknowledge the importance of self-discipline, very few do anything to strengthen it. To cultivate our best selves, we have to look at ourselves in the mirror and start taking ownership. Having a rhythm and routine to our planned daily disciplines.

Self-discipline manifests inner strength, self-confidence, respect and satisfaction. It's what strengthens us to continue on course, no matter what obstacles arise. If we choose to eat healthily every day, for instance, we're more likely to give time to keeping fit, too.

Don't wait: make a commitment to yourself, for yourself. You could start with anything – maybe taking just 30 minutes a day to study, exercise, develop new skills, or focus on spiritual growth or meditation.

Enjoy the process of strengthening your self-discipline muscles.

DEVELOPING ATTENTION TO DETAIL

When you pay attention to detail,
the big picture will take care of itself.

Georges St-Pierre,
Canadian mixed martial artist

DEVELOPING ATTENTION TO DETAIL

The quality of our work is a reflection of how attentive we've been.
It takes hard work to cultivate focus with all the distractions we battle each day. In our personal and professional lives, we're bombarded with a constant feed of information, noise and entertainment. It's time to gain control of our attention and resources. The more detail-orientated we are, the fewer opportunities we'll miss.

Daily habits like embracing a personal routine, noticing personal details about other people, prioritising quality over quantity, limiting distractions, making lists, getting organised and being truly in the moment will help us to develop our attention to detail.

CARPE DIEM

Wake up and live now.

Bob Marley,
Jamaican singer and songwriter

CARPE DIEM

What challenges will we overcome today? What lessons will we learn?
Do we really want to look back on our week and realise we've achieved nothing, or not been present in enjoying each moment?

As American author Napoleon Hill put it: "Don't wait. The time will never be just right." Today will only happen once; we will never get the opportunity to make the most of it again. Will we make the most of every moment in the next 24 hours? Can we be confident we're doing our best with each passing hour?

WHAT IS CONNECTION?

Connection forms an energy. It's not just a relationship in which a person or thing is linked to another – it's a power that prevails when a being feels seen, heard, understood and valued; a pure unconscious feeling born of offering and accepting without judgment. The miracle that is connection gives us strength and nourishment.

Without being attentive, we cannot make a true connection. Our ability to communicate and connect with the world around us impacts every area of our life. It's what determines whether we thrive or dwindle.

One of the keys to connection is being able to relate with people. If we want to make a difference in this world and inspire others to do the same we must understand the awesome power of empathy – something that can never be replicated with connections based only on technology.

Those who reap success are the ones who continue not only to grow in intellect, but those who continually study the art of cultivating rich relationships. Through empathy, their ability to work with people and grow trust means they can unite vision with value.

BECOMING A BETTER COMMUNICATOR

Good communication is as stimulating as black coffee, and just as hard to sleep after.

Anne Morro Lindbergh,
American author

BECOMING A BETTER COMMUNICATOR

We live in an age where its easy to rely on digital connections to build relationships with others. However, we must not confuse connectivity with human connection.

An integral part of success in our personal and professional lives depends on our effectiveness to communicate in a compelling and influential way with those around us.

To connect with others we have to take the time and energy to develop our skills as communicators. Jim Rohn said: "Take advantage of every opportunity to practice your communication skills so that when important occasions arise, you will have the gift, the style, the sharpness, the clarity, and the emotions to affect other people."

Noticing how we connect with others, how we make them feel, how they respond and react to our messages both verbally and non verbally is essential. By being patient and seeking new ways to express ourselves, we will make deeper connections and be more impactful by making others feel valued.

EXPRESS YOURSELF

Dance like no one is watching.
Sing like no one is listening.
Love like you've never been hurt and
live like it's heaven on Earth.

Mark Twain,
writer

EXPRESS YOURSELF

To express ourselves is to discover ourselves. But we can only truly express our feelings, views and values when we liberate ourselves from being "people pleasers" and escape the fear that others will judge us.

There's a fine line between expressing with confidence and arrogance, so we need to maintain a thread of humility. Have the confidence to be your authentic self.

Through speaking out, we can free our minds and connect with the here and now. Whether through creation or verbalising, self-expression can combat stress by helping us feel more complete, conveying our feelings and in turn helping us to connect the space between the real and the imagined self.

Try writing down the different ways in which you enjoy expressing yourself and make it your goal to achieve one of them today.

LOVE YOURSELF FIRST

Love yourself first and everything else falls into line. You really have to love yourself to get anything done in this world.

Lucille Ball,
American actor

LOVE YOURSELF FIRST

It's all too easy to base our self-worth on what other people think. But self-worth is meant to be about how we feel about ourselves.

It can be dangerous to allow other people's opinions to determine how we feel about ourselves. The idea that another's perception of you is more important than your own can be an empty way to approach life.

We have to love and respect ourselves; but it takes courage to consider ourselves in a positive way, and to forgive ourselves for past mistakes.

To love yourself isn't vain: it's crucial to finding soundness of mind in a world that proliferates images and ideas that can feel like they're pushing you into being something you're not. A person has to look past the mirror (or the screen) and make sure they are loving the person, not the reflection.

We can choose to be brave and true to who we are, no matter what we think the opinions of others might be. We all deserve to be happy, and to live a life we're genuinely excited about.

Write a list of five things you love about the real you, and place it somewhere you'll see it, – perhaps on a screensaver or on a Post It note, stuck to a mirror.

TRUE BEAUTY

You are not your body and hair-style,
but your capacity for choosing well.
If your choices are beautiful,
so too will you be.

Epictetus,
Greek Stoic philosopher

TRUE BEAUTY

In a world where it seems everyone pushes an unrealistic and unattainable notion of beauty, it's so easy to feel disillusioned about who we really are.

We can often forget that we have a choice: we can switch ourselves off from outside messages that can erode our authenticity.

So, what is real beauty?

Beauty is a choice. It doesn't depend on good genes, or surgery. Making a conscious effort to not poison our bodies, spirits and minds is the route to growing gracefully, and in a way that's true to our unique selves.

True beauty radiates from our souls when we lovingly share our passions, and when we're happy and content in our own skin.

LOOK AFTER YOU
FOR ME

If you don't love yourself,
you cannot love others.
You will not be able to love others.
If you have no compassion for yourself
then you are not able of developing
compassion for others.

Dalai Lama

LOOK AFTER YOU
FOR ME

The body we are born with is the only home we'll have for our time here on earth. It's up to us to build our home on loving, strong foundations by loving and nourishing our bodies and minds.

Spirituality may mean something different to each of us, but finding a sense of inner peace in whatever way works for us creates a safe house when the outside world is uncertain.

We have to be compassionate towards ourselves – feed our minds, bodies and spirits with the love and kindness we would offer our best friends. It's only by looking after ourselves that we can do more for others.

Write a list of daily self-care tasks you could do that tend to your mind, body and spirit.

IT'S OK TO CRY

We need never be ashamed of our tears.

Charles Dickens,
writer

IT'S OK TO CRY

How often do you let yourself cry?
Why do we so often mask what we're feeling with an "I'm fine, don't worry"?
Why is crying often seen as weakness?

Showing emotion shows you care. It's beneficial to cry when we feel like it: let sad things make you sad. Crying is an aid to experience our most profound feelings. As Jim Rohn said, "The walls we build around us to keep sadness out also keeps out the joy.".

Let's give ourselves permission to cry and heal. The fact that we're feeling at all makes us alive. We can be brave and ask for help when we need it. When we're ready, we'll be smiling again.

Life is a journey of happiness and tears; we have to feel sadness to know its opposite. There is a reason behind every tear we shed.

PRACTICING HUMILITY

Pride makes us artificial;
humility makes us real.

Thomas Merton,
writer and monk

PRACTICING HUMILITY

Practicing humility means we share from our hearts, not our egos.
Constantly trying to prove ourselves to others is tiring and unfulfilling.

Boastful talk can only drain positivity and hinder our connection with the world around us.

It's much more impactful and less tiring to be a quietly confident person, and one who does not seek the approval of others. Dr Tom Barrett reminds us: "Awesome talent worn with humility is always attractive."

Humility makes us secure and authentic; as well as less stressed and angry. Resist the temptations of the ego to show off – instead, let someone else have the glory. We'll feel far more joy in life when we realise we have nothing to prove.

THINGS COME
AND GO

In the process of letting go,
you will lose many things from the past,
but you will find yourself.

Deepak Chopra,
American-Indian author

THINGS COME AND GO

We come into this world with nothing and we leave with nothing.
All we have is here and now. It's utterly liberating to realise the importance
of just being; and not continuously wanting.

The art of "letting go" is an invitation to abandon unhealthy attachments to
ideas, possessions and experiences; setting ourselves free from negative
influences so that we can truly enjoy life.

If we stay anchored in the past, we risk missing out on new opportunities.
Some things in life aren't meant to last; and often the changes we don't
want are the changes we need to develop and grow. Moving out of our
comfort zone can be painful, but it's worth it to escape things in our lives
that no longer belong there.

Peace and wisdom come from accepting what is, letting go of what was
and having hope in what is to come.

Don't let your past paralyse you: your history is not a part of your destiny.

LEARNING TO FORGIVE OFTEN

The weak can never forgive.
Forgiveness is the attribute of the strong.

Mahatma Gandhi,
Indian activist

LEARNING TO FORGIVE OFTEN

One trait that won't change our past but will certainly change our future is the power to forgive.

A forgiving spirit can convert anger and hurt into healing and peace. Holding on to resentment for others and anger towards ourselves only puts the brakes on our personal growth and happiness. Forgiveness is available to all of us; and is vital to helping overcome negativity and conflict.

It takes time to forgive the pain others have caused us; but it's something we must realise can help us in our own self-preservation – something that can help set us free and move on.

We have a choice whether we carry the burden of resentment or not. Why would we not live each day with a forgiving spirit?

Don't judge, forgive.

REACHING
NEW HEIGHTS

Associate with men of good quality
if you esteem your own reputation;
for it is better to be alone
than in bad company.

George Washington,
First President of the United States

REACHING NEW HEIGHTS

Who are the people in your life that you feel better for spending time in the presence of? Who makes you feel good about yourself? Who inspires rather than discourages you?

Life is too short for us not to spend time with the people who bring out the best in us. A true friend – one who knows our strengths and weaknesses; who guides and supports us – knows how to make us smile in good times and bad. They help us develop our self esteem by holding higher standards for themselves and the people around them. They tell us the truth when we need to hear it the most; and give us perspective when we find it hard to see the bigger picture.

Be grateful for the blessing that is true friendship.

BECOMING A
BETTER LISTENER

You cannot truly listen to anyone and do anything else at the same time.

M. Scott Peck,
American psychiatrist and author

BECOMING A
BETTER LISTENER

We often act like the way in which we communicate is a rabid sprint.
Do you find yourself racing to finish others' sentences, interrupting them when they haven't had a chance to even formulate what they're saying?

It doesn't help that we're living in a culture that focuses on being busy – a mad dash to use every second of our day.

Effective listening is to be conscious of this bad habit; and has to be coupled with empathy. It's about being content to listen instead of just anticipating our opportunity to be heard.

Taking some time to breathe and truly listen makes us not only calmer, but far more pleasurable to be around.

When we focus on listening we connect with others on a deeper level. We all enjoy spending time with those who truly listen; who ask questions. Everyone needs to feel valued and respected. Seek out the feelings and emotions behind another's words in their time, not yours.

We have two ears and one mouth for a reason.

NURTURE COMPASSION

People will forget what you said,
people will forget what you did,
but people will never forget
how you made them feel.

Maya Angelou,
writer and civil rights activist

NURTURE COMPASSION

Compassion is defined as "a strong feeling of sympathy for people
who are suffering and a desire to help them." It's about understanding
and accepting that another's struggles and dilemmas are just as real and
as painful as our own, if not more so.

When we start taking life too seriously, even a small act of compassion
and a grateful response can allow us to bring our attention back to the
things that matter most.

Focusing on what matters to someone else can make a massive difference
to them and to us, and help us gain perspective. We feel more gratitude
for what we have in our own lives and help someone else in the process.

CHOOSE TO ACT
WITH KINDESS

Service to others is the rent you pay
for your room here on earth.

Muhammad Ali,
boxer

CHOOSE TO ACT WITH KINDESS

People walk in and out of your life every day, from a stranger on the street you'll never see again to a friend you've known since childhood. With every person we encounter, we have a chance to share kindheartedness – to value each and every individual we come into contact with.

If we treat people with disrespect and hostility on our way up, we will inevitably have to meet them on the way down.

We could become someone's mentor, listen to their story, forgive a person we've born a grudge towards, buy a stranger's coffee, pay someone an honest compliment, or just smile at someone.

Small acts of kindness have a big impact.

KEEP CHEERING

The unselfish effort to bring cheer to others
will be the beginning of a happier life
for ourselves.

Helen Keller,
author, political activist and lecturer

KEEP CHEERING

Watching others succeed is not always a great feeling, especially if we feel things aren't looking so great for ourselves. But true friends are selfless.

A generous spirit practices empathy. A virtuous person will look out for their friends, be moved by their failure and excited for their successes. True joy is found in helping and supporting others to succeed and grow.

We can all choose to put aside jealousy, selfishness and control. Actively cheer and celebrate the advancement of friends and family. Supporting another's success and light won't ever reduce or dim yours.

There's enough sunshine for everyone.

GRUMPY VS. GRATEFUL

Gratitude is the healthiest of all human emotions. The more you express gratitude for what you have, the more likely you will have even more to express gratitude for.

Zig Ziglar,
motivational speaker and author

GRUMPY VS. GRATEFUL

Think of all that you have to be grateful for in your life.
That you are alive: you can feel the daylight on your skin, you have the time
to enjoy being, and doing the things that make you happy, if you let yourself.
Think of the little things: the stranger who smiled and acknowledged you today,
the blue skies, the running water, the fresh vegetables, the music that lifted your
spirits, the friend who called to just see how your day was going.

Gratitude reduces feelings of jealousy, depression and unhealthy wanting for
things: it makes our memories sweeter, lets us experience good feelings and
helps us bounce back from stress. There is a strong connection between gratitude,
inner peace and feeling alive.

It's crucial for optimism, confidence and positivity; for letting go of unhelpful
materialistic yearnings, and jealousies we don't need. Let us identify what we
have, identify the people who have blessed us, and remember to thank them.

Leading researcher on gratitude Robert Emmons suggests three ways we can
make an effort to start bringing a little more gratitude into our lives: a morning
meditation, counting our blessings at bedtime or keeping a gratitude journal.
Perhaps start by writing down a description of three things you are grateful
for today.

LOVE ALWAYS

The beginning of love is to let
those we love be perfectly themselves,
and not to twist them to fit our own image.
Otherwise we love only the reflection
of ourselves we find in them.

Thomas Merton,
writer and monk

LOVE ALWAYS

Who doesn't want a life filled with love?
Love is broad. It will be different for everyone we meet. We can love a friend, a partner, a family member all as much as each other but all in different ways.

Loathing and resentment only hinder us. When we disagree with others, embracing compassion, admiration, respect, humility and understanding can only make the situation better.

Love is like an echo; the love we send out will amplify and radiate its way back to us. Commit to being a source of love through your attitude, acts of kindness, choices and eagerness to serve others. C.S. Lewis wrote: "Love is unselfishly choosing for another's highest good."

Love is an essential aspect of a prosperous life. It drives out fear and darkness. Share, care, give and receive.

Let others be who they are: unconditionally love and accept them.

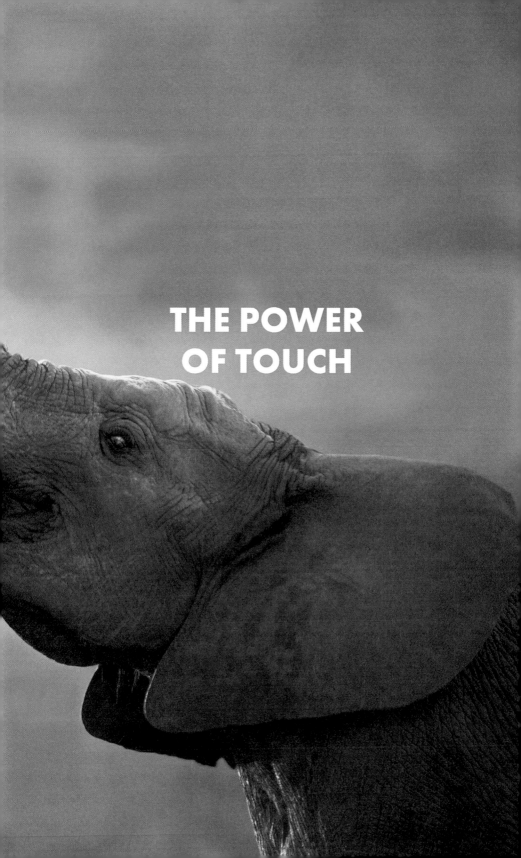

THE POWER
OF TOUCH

Too often we underestimate
the power of a touch...

Leo Buscaglia,
American author and motivational speaker

THE POWER OF TOUCH

In our guarded culture of tech-based communication, we often miss out on a powerful component of the human experience – touch.

We have a primal need for touch: it impacts our physical, mental and emotional health, and quite literally shapes the way we go through life.

A study conducted by researchers at Berkeley examined professional NBA teams, noting how often the basketball players interacted through celebratory touches — fist bumps, chest bumps, high fives, taps on the rear end —and came up with a number per game for each team.
The teams that had more celebratory touches in the first half of the season won more games in the second half of the season. The power of their touch created a sense of team work, energy and enthusiasm; which led them to success. Don't underestimate this powerful form of non verbal communication in your personal and professional life.

Make mini connections happen where appropriate: offer a high five to a gym buddy, or a simple hug to a friend you meet for coffee.

WHAT IS CREATION?

Creation is the result of thought, action and process.
Although in the 21st century, number-crunching work and similar tasks are far more efficiently carried out by computers than man; tech still falls far short of humans when it comes to creativity.

Creativity is impossible without paying attention to, and connecting with, the world around us. It takes courage and embracing vulnerability to share that creativity, though. Learn to enjoy the thrill of risk-taking and experimenting; relish growth through making mistakes.

Be liberated in the thought that we, as people, were created for creation.

The only thing worse than being blind
is having sight but no vision.

Helen Keller,
author, political activist and lecturer

BE A VISIONARY

Vision is a more powerful tool than a hope or dream,
because of its clarity and precision.

A vision helps us create a plan, set a goal, make defined decisions.
It helps us engage those around us when we share our vision; and
connect with others. We thrive in communities, especially when we
can really imagine our own roles within those communities and what
we're working together towards.

If we have a vision, let's use it to inspire our actions and enforce our
objectives. Acknowledge the difficulties and have faith in your vision.

Vision brings inspiration, and inspiration forges vision.

TAKING OWNERSHIP

The victim mindset
dilutes the human potential.
By not accepting personal responsibility
for our circumstances,
we greatly reduce our power
to change them.

Steve Maraboli,
Speaker, author, and behavioural scientist

TAKING OWNERSHIP

Our life, heart and happiness is our responsibility alone.

Of course, life's traumas and heartbreaks aren't always our own doing. It's not our fault if we get cheated on, but it's up to us to figure out how we're going to take that pain and overcome it.

It's dangerous to get stuck in a victim mindset. Power comes from loving ourselves enough to take ownership.

We are a product of our decisions not our situations. No matter how we may feel in the moment, let us be accountable for our daily decisions.

The things we can control are our attitude and reactions.

When we face uncertainty we can keep in mind the Serenity Prayer that American theologian Reinhold Niebuhr once wrote "God, grant me the serenity to accept the things I cannot change, courage to change the things I can, and wisdom to know the difference."

GREATER QUALITIES

We all have our imperfections.
But I'm human, and you know,
it's important to concentrate on other
qualities besides outer beauty.

Beyonce Knowles,
American singer-songwriter

GREATER QUALITIES

Everyone believes they have shortfalls in some shape or form,
and it's easy to let them form a blaming mindset – maybe they feel they aren't smart enough, or resentful about the family they were born into.

Whatever we perceive to be our faults, remember that we can always develop our own qualities that have no bearing on our background or genetics.

We can choose our own qualities that really enable us to thrive: choose to be gracious, perhaps; to be generous, respectful, honest, humble, kind.

ATTITUDE EFFECTS
EVERYTHING

Your attitude,
not your aptitude,
will determine your altitude

Zig Ziglar,
motivational speaker and author

ATTITUDE EFFECTS EVERYTHING

Austrian neurologist, psychiatrist and Holocaust survivor Viktor E. Frankl wrote, "Everything can be taken from a man but one thing: the last of human freedoms – to choose one's attitude in any given set of circumstances, to choose one's own way."

The attitude we cultivate will either make us or break us.

We can decide to view life as a series of opportunities to learn and grow from, rather than a sequence of difficulties and failures. Nothing is lost unless we choose to quit.

No matter what happens, choose to arm yourself with a positive attitude.

Do what you can,
with what you have,
where you are.

Theodore Roosevelt,
twenthy sixth President of the United States

ACT NOW

Why not be a "do it now" kind of person? Decide to do something over nothing; not letting fear lead to inertia.

Worry and procrastination are the enemies of a productive life. Fear is nothing but a waste of creativity. Do you want to be a slave to your future or a champion of your best life?

Author Stephen King reminds us: "Amateurs sit and wait for inspiration, the rest of us get up and go to work." When we choose to act now we will inspire others to do the same. However big or small the act may be, don't wait. What action can you take that will move you one step closer to your goal?

Make the most of your time. Productivity boosts self confidence.

SEARCH FOR SHOOTING STARS

One of the greatest values of mentors is the ability to see ahead what others cannot see and to help them navigate a course to their destination.

John C. Maxwell,
American author, speaker and pastor

SEARCH FOR SHOOTING STARS

A shooting star is a bright, wondrous light in the dark space of the night sky. Just as we delight in spotting those rare, miraculous sights; search among those we know for people who we admire for facing adversity fearlessly.

Those people are our shooting stars, right here on earth. Seek their wisdom, ask how they made their decisions, overcame their obstacles, and battled against fears.

Whether it's a character in our favourite story or the bravest person we have in our life, soak up all we can from them. A shooting star will give us the opportunity to discover ourselves from their own wisdom.

Keep an open mind: we can gain so much from having someone to ask, an ear to listen or a nudge in the right direction.

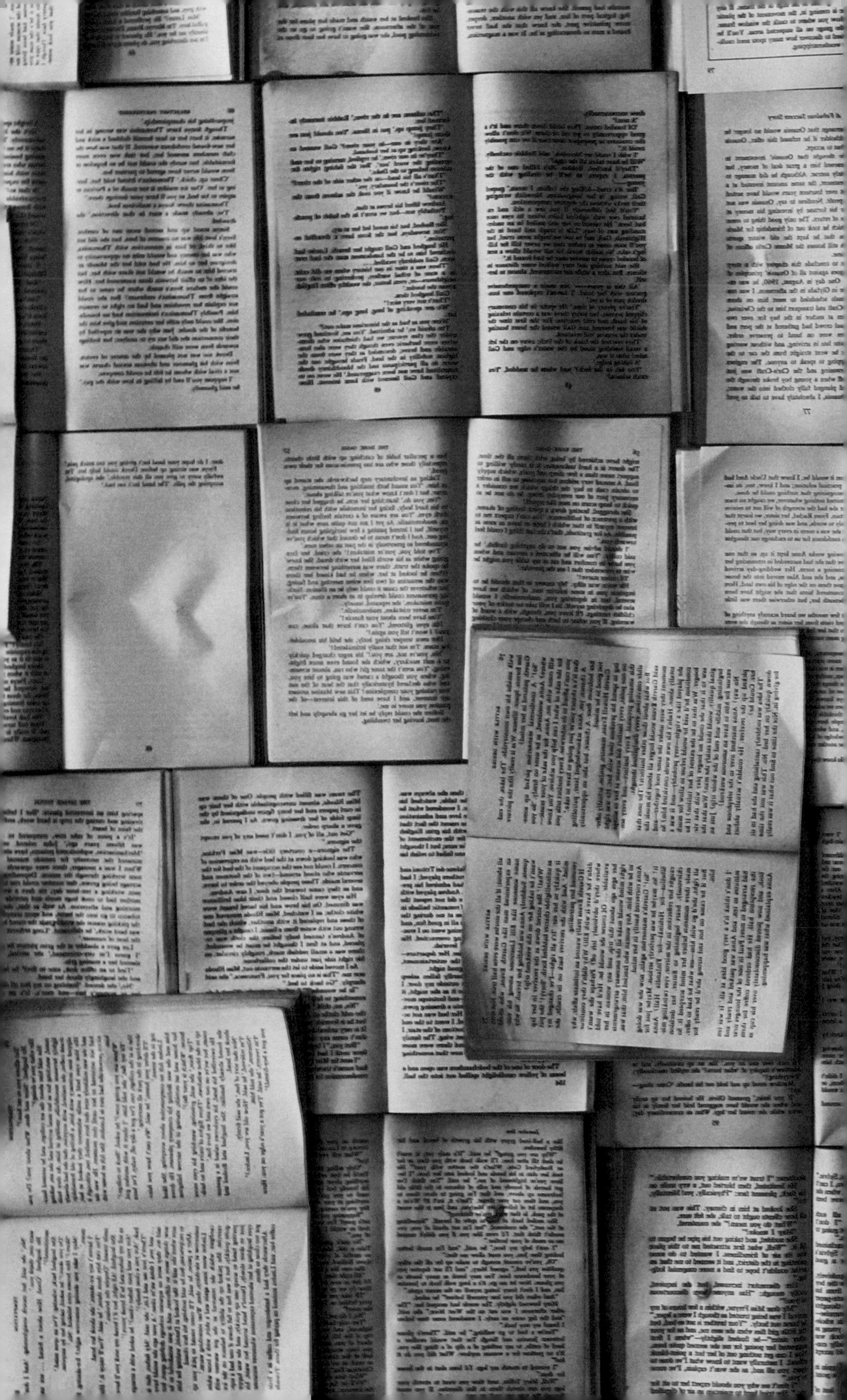

**REMAIN A
HUMBLE STUDENT**

Shall I tell you a secret of a true scholar?
It is this: every man I meet is my master in
some point and in that I learn from him.

Ralph Waldo Emerson,
American writer, philosopher and poet

REMAIN A
HUMBLE STUDENT

One of the most wonderful gifts in life is that we never have to stop learning. Everything that we are is a sum of the books we've read, the thoughts we've processed, experiences we've had and the people we've shared time with.

To be creative is to remain a student and allow ourselves to continuously evolve.

We all believe from time to time that we know it all, but there will always be someone wiser and more skilled we can learn from.

Seeking out mentors and knowledge is the place to begin, but we will only be truly successful by taking the responsibility to respond with action to the wisdom we learn.

Always stay humble and be open to changing your perspective.

LITTLE THINGS
ADD UP

It's the little details that are vital.
Little things make big things happen.

John Wooden,
American basketball player

LITTLE THINGS ADD UP

We all know the little things add up. Success is an accumulation of small positive actions. Even seemingly insignificant actions build to form a colossal cumulative effect.

As Jeff Olson explains in his book The Slight Edge: "Every day, in every moment, you get to exercise choices that will determine whether or not you will become a great person, living a great life.

"Greatness is not something predetermined, predestined or carved into your fate by forces beyond your control. Greatness is always in the moment of the decision."

Choose right over easy with every action in your day, and observe how these little things transform over time. Make simple positive choices that seem easy, but often aren't: rising early, making your bed, investing in yourself, resisting the urge to play or procrastinate instead of getting to work.

Pay attention: take deep breaths, and consistently make small positive steps in the direction of your dreams.

LIFE IS A PROCESS

The good life is a process,
not a state of being.
It is a direction not a destination.

Carl Rogers,
American psychologist

LIFE IS A PROCESS

There will always be someone more talented than you – more athletic, smarter, or prettier – but no one is "better" than you. You are unique and special. There never has, and never will be, another person just like you.

Don't let comparison destroy your own joy.

Who we are and what we do is is completely up to us. That's a daunting, but also a liberating thought. No matter where the rest of the crowd is heading, we don't have to follow.

Enjoy the baby steps, for they are what make up the big steps of life.

This is a journey, not a destination. Keep on enjoying life and doing your thing.

LEARN TO LOVE
THE RIDE

Just play.
Have fun.
Enjoy the game.

Michael Jordan,
American former professional basketball player

LEARN TO LOVE THE RIDE

Learn to love the ride and allow yourself to screw up.
Living life to the full is about actively reaching for new experiences,
without always worrying about what's around the corner.

To live an abundant life we must be aware of our ability to endure
calamities, frustrations, setbacks and disappointments with a good heart.

Decide to accept failure for what it actually is – a very natural part of
human experience. If we are too afraid to screw up now and then we
will continue on the path to a mediocre life.

Life is not about changing the past or presuming the future: it's about
doing, being, becoming and then letting go.

Don't be afraid of being thrown in at the deep end, it's how we'll learn
to swim. Let us keep on overcoming life's challenges reaching for our
full potential.

Whatever happens, be a lover of your fate: live it, love it, learn from it!

CALMNESS IS CONTAGIOUS

There are only two types of player-
those who keep their nerves
under control and win championships,
and those who do not.

Harry Vardon,
professional golfer

CALMNESS IS CONTAGIOUS

It's so easy to let our emotions run riot when turbulent times hit.
It's ok to feel overwhelmed at times, but it's in times of chaos and
upheaval that we have to remind ourselves the value of self-control,
grace and poise.

Choose not to feed paranoia, irrational thoughts and responses.
Calmness is contagious. People will be empowered by the leader who
looks their problems dead on and says: "We can handle this!"

It takes inner strength, patience and practice to stay calm in times of
calamity. Learn to control your emotions, develop your patience, grow
your self confidence and give silent strength to others.

Pride is a spiritual cancer:
it eats up the very possibility of love or
contentment, or even common sense

C.S. Lewis,
British writer

FIGHT EGO

As a cloud blocks the sunlight, ego casts a shadow over your true spirit.
We can often find ourselves falling for an image that will impress others – maybe a job title, material possessions, or even the people we associate with. Ego loves to mask what matters most and substitute it for what does not.

Take time to think about what drives you. Do you feel your value is in being productive? Do you want to impress others, or prove your ability to yourself? Is your value in being you?

Choose a kind, positive attitude over ego; the former makes you unique and brilliant, the latter just serves to stop you truly connecting with the world.

BEYOND YOUR KNOWLEDGE

Knowledge speaks, but wisdom listens.

Jimi Hendrix,
guitarist, songwriter

BEYOND YOUR KNOWLEDGE

Knowledge is the information we have acquired through experience and education; it gives us the ability to formulate our own, unique opinions.

Being knowledgeable doesn't necessarily make us right. It can, however, feed the ego – and as such, breed arrogance. Everyone has the right to their own opinion. Through listening to others – even those with opinions we don't agree with – we expand what we understand in turn.

We are not all that we know. Define yourself as a person who is open to those who oppose what you "know." Listen to others – they might change how you see the world.

Be a discoverer. Be humble, be willing to admit it when you realise you were wrong.

FINDING PEACE
WITH PROGRESSION

Stop beating yourself up.
You are a work in progress;
which means you
get there a little at a time,
not all at once.

Anonymous

FINDING PEACE
WITH PROGRESSION

The dual need for perfection and inner peace is a contradiction.
When we find ourselves wanting something to be perfect, we're heading down a dead end street. Instead of being content and grateful for what we have, and the way things are, we focus on what is wrong and our desperation to fix it.

Instead, focus on progression with the knowledge and comfort that even if we come off course, the path is still within our reach and we're still heading in the right direction.

Remember to let go of our desire to be in control of every situation, and find peace in doing our best with what we have right now.

Pursue your passion, find your purpose, live in a mindset of constant progression.

GO THE DISTANCE

Genius is 1% inspiration,
99% perspiration.

Thomas Edison,
American inventor

GO THE DISTANCE

As author and psychologist Angela Lee Duckworth said:
"Enthusiasm is common. Endurance is rare."

An essential quality of any successful person is the ability to endure in the face of obstacles: to take stock in times of hardship and simply keep going through disappointment, pain and betrayal.

Be the individual who doesn't rely on luck, but hard work, diligence and honesty. You can be a product of fortitude, strength and resilience.

Always do your best.
What you plant now,
you will harvest later.

Og Mandino,
American author

DO YOUR BEST
AND THEN LET GO

We can decide – today – to give everything our best shot.
If we want to improve our confidence, achieve our goals and never feel the regret of "what if" when we look back on our life, then let's do our own personal best each and every day.

Author and speaker Brian Tracy put it well: "Happiness and self-confidence come naturally when you feel you are moving and progressing toward becoming the very best person you can possibly be."

Have you noticed how improving in just one area of your life boosts your confidence?

Take action to build your confidence: allow your existing qualities to shine through while you develop other areas, focus on your strengths, and not your restrictions. Be daring, determined and tenacious.

Do your best everyday and then let go: that's enough.

KEEPING
A LIGHT HEART

Do not take life too seriously.
You will never get out of it alive.

Elbert Hubbard,
American author

KEEPING A LIGHT HEART

Keeping a light heart is dependent on our willingness to accept life as it is, instead of trying to control other people and external circumstances.

We get frustrated when things don't play out the way we imagined, and it's easy to lose perspective over the little things – someone saying the wrong thing, being late for an appointment, the internet going down, having to queue.

We could all learn from not taking life so seriously. When we live with a lighter heart, we have more fun living.

Let's practice letting go of our expectations. We'll be pleasantly surprised how life becomes less of a battle and more of a waltz. When we learn to laugh at ourselves, we can see the funny side of the situation.

The reality is that good and bad stuff is always going to happen, but by practicing letting things go we'll lighten up our whole life and fill it with a lot more laughter.

Live life to the full with a light heart and a sweet spirit.

BALANCE

Work, love and play are the
great balance wheels of man's being.

Orison Swett Marden,
American author

BALANCE

Taking anything too far can ultimately lead to its destruction.
Finding balance in our lives brings contentment.

Our fast-paced modern culture can be antithetical to maintaining a balanced life.It's easy to burn out when there are so many opportunities, and so much pressure to do everything, wherever we are, all the time.

Before we know it, our days are crammed from start to finish and we have no energy for what we need or want.

Finding balance, order and rhythm doesn't come naturally to most of us, and can be made all the more difficult when the hardships of life unfold. Give yourself time to slow down, breath, take stock and heal.

Staying balanced is something to work at for self preservation: establish some boundaries, turn your phone off at night, take up a new creative pursuit, know your limits, schedule in regular down time. Protect your time and energy.

Living with balance takes time, and often a mental shift on how you approach life. We're all different, and we all have individual priorities. Identify and work towards YOUR own personal balance.

None of us are getting out of here alive.
So please stop treating yourself
like an afterthought.
Eat the delicious food.
Walk in the sunshine.
Jump in the ocean.
Say the truth that you're carrying in your
heart like hidden treasure.
Be silly.
Be kind.
Be weird.
There is no time for anything else.

Anthony Hopkins,
Actor, director and producer

ENJOY, RELAX

The Dalai Lama said, "We are human beings not human doings."
Most of us put off making time to just chill, and just be, until our list of things to do is complete. That list will always be endless.

Technology doesn't help as emails and the rest pile up, reminding us even on our days off that there's always work to be done.

But periods of relaxation will help our workflow, and we'll become more productive and efficient. We'll feel far more calmness within ourselves if we block out just ten minutes every morning to collect ourselves, and set ourselves up for the day ahead.

Allow ourselves the time to laugh, to contemplate, to be ourselves: ignore the pressure of always having to "do".

THE BEST IS YET
TO COME

You can't go back
and change the beginning,
but you can start where you are
and change the ending.

C.S. Lewis,
British writer

THE BEST IS YET TO COME

Take time to reflect on how much our life has changed throughout our time here on earth already. Consider all the obstacles we never thought we could overcome, the things that once kept us awake at night but which fell away into the black hole of time.

How much stronger, more beautiful and wiser we have become through all our trials and tribulations. Our mistakes, and the difficult situations we've faced have made us smarter.

We've learnt so many lessons already that we can apply to the adventure in front of us. If we learn from our mistakes, then every day we can become a better version of ourselves.

Whether you're at rock bottom or at what might feel like the peak of your life's summit, keep building on the foundations for your best life.

Some of the best days of our lives haven't happened yet.

FURTHER READING

Please consider these titles for a deeper understanding on some of the topics covered in Being the Real You.

- The Power Of Now, Ekhart Tolle.
- The 7 Habits Of Highly Effective People, Steven R Covey
- I Love Me: The Science of Self Love, David R Hamilton
- Solve For Happy, Mo Gawdat
- What To Say When You Talk To Yourself, Shad Helmstetter
- Deep Work, Cal Newport
- Grit, Angela Duckworth
- The Gifts of Imperfection: Let Go of Who You Think You're Supposed to Be and Embrace Who You Are, Brené Brown
- Daring Greatly: How the Courage to Be Vulnerable Transforms the Way We Live, Love, Parent, and Lead, Brené Brown
- The Magic of Thinking Big, David J. Schwartz
- The Slight Edge, Jeff Olsen
- Ego is The Enemy, Ryan Holiday
- The Art of Exceptional Living, Jim Rohn
- The Happiness Project, Gretchen Rubin
- The War of Art: Break Through the Blocks and Win Your Inner Creative Battles, Steven Pressfield

ABOUT THE AUTHOR

Sarah Ellen Masters is a personal trainer-turned-designer currently living in Dorset who's passionate about inspiring others on life's journey.

She began her studies in Graphic Web & Media Design at Southampton Solent University in September 2016, taking what she'd learned from training about the importance of inspiring positivity and confidence in her clients into an arena where she could use visual communication and creativity to reach more people.

At the heart of Sarah Ellens' drive is an ambition to make self-development material more accessible – especially to young adults who struggle with peer pressure and social media-driven expectations. Her vision was to inspire more than just her clients, mentally, physically and spiritually.

The author has long enjoyed reading broadly around personal growth, and attending related seminars on the subject of personal growth. These have given her the tenacity and courage to be herself; and the realisation of how easy it is to lose perspective on the important things in life while being distracted by things that aren't.

ACKNOWLEDGEMENTS

THANK YOU TO MY SHOOTING STARS LISTED HERE,
YOU INSPIRE ME EVERYDAY.

To Siri Lieungh, Paul Cole, Matt Ridgeway and Andy Waring for your faith in me and my dream, your valuable time and suggestions during the early stages of this book were indispensable.

To Radim Malinic for leading the way, your passion for design is contagious.

To Kevin Bishop for all your time and patience on helping me cultivate the fundementals of my creative skillset.

To Brent Meheux for everything you've taught me. You are a Powerhouse of creative knowledge and I feel so blessed to have been a part of WMD (Weapons of Mass Destruction).

To Chris Venables for never beating around the bush and for sharing your love of design.

To Sharon Bott aka Big Blue Love for empowering me to create and for all your valuable time spent reading my manuscripts.

To dear friends that are always there to hang out, encourage and listen; Rachel Scott, Edoardo Rainaldo, Jade Bennett, Clare Marie Nicholas, Gail Turner, Savannah Turner, Daisy Alice Emily Burr, Paul Hardiman, Cornel Ene, Nicole Cuthbert, Rose Cole, Lynne Davey, Elaine Hibell and Julie Richards.

To Edward Baylis for always checking in and keeping me sane in moments of panic.

To Barry Phillips for sharing your wisdom on self development books and for all your support.

To Everton McCloud for giving your perspective on the initial drafts of Being the Real You.

To The Communication Guys: Dr. Tom Barrett and Tim Downs. Your work is a weekly source of inspiration that makes this world a better and more connected place. Your podcasts were many a starting point for the research of this book.

Finally to my family; Helen, Gary, James and Becky for all your love, kindness and endurance. Thank you.